Saved by the Dead

Saved by the Dead

poems by

Robert Cooperman

Liquid Light Press

Premium Chapbook First Edition

Copyright © 2018

ISBN-10: 0-9985487-3-1

ISBN-13: 978-0-9985487-3-9

Liquid Light Press

poetry for the heart

www.liquidlightpress.com

Book Design: M. D. Friedman
Author Photo: Beth Cooperman

For my brother Jeff and for Brian D.,
and as always, for my darling, Beth.

Contents

The Jerry Garcia T-Shirt

I throw it on because it's light
as a guitar pick this day of July heat.
Also, I loved the man, though
I doubt I'd have known what
to say to him had we been stuck
in an elevator together.

By the time I reach the copy shop,
I've forgotten I'm wearing it,
when a clerk, a kid no more
than twenty, stares at the shirt
to make me fear I've spilled
something disgusting on it,
like my mortal enemy, ketchup.

"The Grateful Dead, right?"
the kid demands, and I agree.
"Awesome," he gushes.
Normally I'd have verbally
cut him like Zorro for that cliché,
but I can forgive almost anything,
if it's about that glorious band:

unlike the guy who owns the local
New York style pizza parlor,
and who, when he saw me
wearing that shirt demanded
if I was going to the Furthur show,
and when I confessed "No,"

his hurt look at my lack
of commitment akin to a kid's
who's been told by his dad
that Santa Claus doesn't exist.

Seeing Ghosts

Pulling into our light rail stop
to pick up my wife,
I blink and blink again:

Jerry Garcia's standing on the curb—
the same grizzled hair, beard,
the same granny shades,
the right height, the build
of a bear too busy eating
to bother with hibernation.

All that's missing,
the guitar case, and the tunes
that floated about his head.
I can't stop staring, can barely
contain myself from gushing,

"My God, you look just like Garcia."

His answering scowl tells me
he's more tired of hearing that
than of having his cheek pinched
by adoring aunts when he was a kid.

By now, my wife has descended
from her train and waves;
I wave back. In our car, I whisper,
"There's a guy over there,
looks just like Jerry Garcia."

"Where?" Beth pivots,
but no one's there, only the air
shimmering like a campfire
when someone tells a ghost story.

The Angels and the Dead

I was running later than the White Rabbit,
to meet friends at the old Fillmore East,
to see the Grateful Dead. In my panic
that I'd miss the show's first notes,
I darted down the Hells Angels' stronghold
on East 3rd, rumored to be a black hole dark star:
anyone who trespassed, never seen again.

A miracle, one of the two shepherds
that guarded the street's ends didn't go for me
with stiletto fangs, but like a wall, there was
the biggest Angel I never wanted to see again.
He grabbed me by my collar, my legs pumping
like a cartoon figure, his chains jangling
like the bridles of an evil knight's charger;
two hammers, I shuddered, slung from his belt
like a gunslinger's brace of .45s;
and more grease in his hair and beard
than in his hog's engine and moving parts.

"Whoa there, little man," he bellowed,
more good humored than I'd expected,
or hoped for. "What's the hurry?"

"I'm late," I gasped, "to see the Dead,"
and waved my ticket. Too late, I realized
he might separate me from that Open Sesame.
But he set me down, told me to enjoy the show.

"Me and my bros will see you there later,"
he confided. I waved my delight
at that charming reunion, and kept running,
glad to escape with all my teeth and ribs

though common courtesy, had he offered
a ride on his Harley, for my grand entrance.

The Night the Dead First Played "Dark Star" at the Old
Fillmore East

Dark star: a black hole.

But to us at the old Fillmore
that night, "Dark Star" meant
the music of the spheres:

Pythagoras might've been up
near the stage, twirling
to the beat the drums laid down
hypnotic as a snake charmer,
the guitars and keyboards weaving,
like the dance of DNA molecules,
the universe forming that night.

Garcia's guitar a pterodactyl
soaring on thermals, diving
for prey just under the surface,
then stroking skyward again
higher and higher, almost more
than music was capable of.

And all the while we swayed
like a field of wind-weaving barley
on this night of pulsing
planets, comets, and stars.

When we left the concert hall,
dawn was turning East Village
buildings the color of doves.

"What the hell was that?"
one friend asked.

"I don't know," I answered,
"but I never wanted it to end."

"And We Bid You Goodnight"——The Fillmore East

For years, the Grateful Dead
closed their shows
with *a capella* versions
of that old gospel hymn
about loving each other
but Jesus loving us best:

The crowd's arms draped
around the shoulders of friends
or complete strangers
and swaying to the melody,
the song sent us into the dawn
with smiles sweet as ice cream.

Maybe we'd stop at Ratner's
for omelets and those tiny,
crunchy, egg washed rolls
that were as good——in their way——
as the Dead; or maybe we'd trudge
to the subway: almost empty,
no maniac with a knife, gun,
or the always rumored axe.

Or on the show's menorah glow,
we'd amble the almost two
hundred blocks to our neighborhood;
trucking along on the soaring
of gorgeous exhaustion,
mauling the lyrics to,

"And We Bid You Goodnight,"
and all the other wonderful songs:
the city blossoming, noisy-insane.

A Friday Night Dinner with My Parents: 1971

After dinner, my dad and I watched
the Knicks. During a time-out, he asked,

"You still got some of that marijuana?"

Wary as a bootlegger around a sniffing
revenuer, I answered, "Why?"

"Roll me a cigarette for later."
When my head stopped spinning
as if I'd smoked a joint in record speed,
I showed him, without lighting up,
how to draw the burning herb into his lungs:
deeper than his suicide Camels.

After the first half, I left for the long
subway ride to my apartment, where
I toked up, settled into my rattan chair,
and set the Grateful Dead on the turntable,
musing over life's, and parents', surprises.

Late Saturday morning, the phone rang.

"Your mother and I," my dad announced,
"had a very nice time after you left.
But don't ever offer me that stuff again,"
he hung up on his wastrel son.

What did I expect, that he'd suddenly
wear tie-dyed t-shirts, pirate bandanas,
and follow the Dead with me in a VW
Microbus he wouldn't accuse
was invented by Hitler?

Watching b-ball together
would have to do.

Marijuana Sauce

Flustered when the pretty counter girl
in her skintight t-shirt
at the local sandwich shop asked,
"Cheese?" on my eggplant sub,
without thinking, I answered,

"Just marijuana sauce," my face
suddenly red, as if I'd toked too much
into my not-as-young-as-they-used-to-be
lungs, and was coughing it all
into the blue and unpolluted sky.

"Marinara sauce!" I corrected,
before I thought she'd heard
that Freudian slip: years since
I'd last indulged.

She sent my order to the cook,
and while handing me my change,
whispered, right out of the Village's
Fillmore East, circa 1969,

"That can be arranged."

I blushed as if she'd proposed
something even more intimate,
and shook my head,

"But thanks for asking," I whispered,
and had a smiling inkling
of my wife's glow, when college guys
hit on her in the university's pool.

Marijuana Sauce, II

I must have subliminally registered
the medicinal dispensary across the street,
because when the sub shop counter-woman—
young as the granny-skirted
twirling hippies at the Old Fillmore East
when the Grateful Dead played all night—
asks what I want on my eggplant sub,

"Marijuana sauce," slips off my tongue.

She stares at me, too old, she's judging,
to have heard of, let alone indulged,
in reefer, weed, ganja, herb, dope,
ookey-dookey, vegetable,
or any of its other myriad names—

almost as many names as Eskimos
have for snow, the Irish for green—
for the marijuana whose aroma
I still find delicious, even if a single toke
makes me cough for an hour or two.

"Marinara sauce," I correct myself,
Beth's turn to stare, never approving
of my imbibing, and wondering now,
I suspect, if I've slipped back
into the pernicious habits
she rescued me from,
with the love of a good woman.

A Question Posed in Anthony's New York Style Pizza:
Denver

I'm in my usual rear booth, in heaven,
with two slices, cheese, and the sports section,
when this kid stands next to my table.

"Yeah?" I try to imitate a Don, but don't have
the requisite goons who'd toss his ass into the gutter.

"Excuse me, Sir," he clears his throat. I start
to reach for my wallet, just to get rid of him,
but it's not money he's after.

"I've been outta the country, and understand grass
is legal? But the dude at the dispensary said
I needed a card, for like, medical marijuana,
since recreational weed ain't sold yet.
Can I borrow your card?" he asks,

and I'm sixteen again, begging an old guy
to buy a buddy and me a pint of cheap scotch.

"Sorry," I swim up from my past, "I don't have one."
He lingers, not believing me, flaps his arms
against his sides at how difficult a simple request
can be, and is gone. And part of me's worried

he'll be waiting, with something hard, heavy,
or sharp: to separate me from the card he believes
I'm too spiteful a geezer to lend him.

The other part's flattered he thinks I'm young
enough at heart to still toke up. But I'm wearing
my Jerry Garcia cap, my Grateful Dead hoodie—
the uniform that wafts me down marijuana lane—

and realize he was acting only on cold logic.

Walking Downtown

Walking downtown
to meet my wife for dinner,
I sense a guy overtaking me,
his shadow hulking, dangerous.

Before I can whirl with my keys,
the aroma of the excellent weed
he's smoking with the panache
of FDR and his cigarette holder
belly dances in my brain.

Then his pungency is past me,
but I can still smell that heady
blend, and I'm floated back
to the old Fillmore East:
the Grateful Dead blasting me
and the rest of the crowd
into space with the first time
most of us heard "Dark Star."

I must be wearing a grin
of supreme psychedelic goofiness
as I saunter into my wife's office,
for Beth smiles, "You look happy,"
innocent of my second-hand high
composed of memories and smoke.

In the Spirit-of-Halloween Store

Skeletons everywhere, and none
jaunty, like the top-hatted dancers
that symbolized the Grateful Dead.
Instead, eyes burn crimson-malevolent,
blood drips from vampire-fangs:
to mix monsters like metaphors.

Jerry Garcia claimed the skeletons
on t-shirts, bumper stickers,
and album covers creeped him out:
shuddering visions of the graveyards
that loomed too large in his life

of watching his father drown
when he was five, getting word
his mother's car had plunged
off a cliff; not to mention
that hatchet and his middle finger.

Anyway, I'm here to buy decorations
for our dinner party: something harmless,
like a jack-o'-lantern, my wife says;
but find ghouls, zombies, vampires,
werewolves, those monstrous skeletons:
I've wandered into an abattoir.

Like Garcia, I've had too much blood
on the wrong side of my skin.
So while his ashes make their eternal,
drifting journey in this cold wind
and freezing, cleansing October rain,
I step outside, empty-handed.

Guys Have It Difficult

Passing one of the park's porta potties
on our morning walk, and seeing three guys
lined up, dancing foot to foot—the universal
gesture of male urinary desperation—Beth says,

"Guys have it difficult," though the lines
for men's rooms at the NBA games
and Grateful Dead shows we used to go to
moved faster than those for the ladies' room.

"I mean," she laughs, "you've got to wait
behind some kid doing his eternal business
at a urinal, and hearing his flow can't be easy,
while the stalls give us privacy, with no
impatient breaths on our spines from someone
who's had way too much to drink,
and who might kill us so he can let fly."

"On the other hand," I counter, this not
one of our more philosophically lofty
morning-constitutional discussions,
"women take so much longer; a miracle
there aren't fights when someone finally
sashays out, her dress and makeup perfect."

"At least," Beth's final, indisputable point,
"we don't do our business in the sink,
like that disgusting guy you complained
about the last time we saw the Dead,
the one who laughed and called you,
'squeamish,' and you shot back with,

"'I'm surprised you know words of more
than one syllable,' and he didn't hit you."
Beth takes my arm, grateful my big, fat
mouth hasn't gotten me beaten up, yet.

Never Trust Anyone Younger Than Thirty

"What a cool t-shirt,"
the cashier gushes: young
and pretty and carefree
as a night of clubbing
and no morning hangover.

I smile, tell her the design—
a pastel tree rising from the bank
of a cleaned up Hudson River—
was painted by Jerry Garcia."

"A local artist?" she asks.

After my head stops vibrating
like those cartoon characters
smacked with skillets,
I sigh, "The lead guitarist
of the Grateful Dead?"

"Oh yeah," she's trying
to placate a good customer now.
"I should've known that."

I relate the incident to a friend,
who tells me, "When I asked
my high school-senior daughter
if she knew who Garcia was,
Zoë scrunched up her nose
and guessed, 'A baseball player?'"

"We are so old," Charles and I agree.

Afterwards, I play an old Dead CD
and dance around the bedroom,
hoping for Beth to come home
and reassure me our best years
are still all ahead of us.

The Nurse Practitioner

"That's so cool," she gushes
over my Jerry Garcia t-shirt,
to put me at ease, while
examining the mole
gnawing at my back.

"My dad used to look just
like him," she goes on,
"and people would demand
his autograph or want him
to play a riff or sing something.
After the first dozen times,
he stopped asking me—
in a snit big as Utah—
'Who the hell's Jerry Garcia?'"

She's done her best
to relax me, and exclaims,
"Oh this . . ." and pronounces
something that sounds toxic
as the most lethal disease
ever to sink its fangs into
half the world's population.

"Liquid nitrogen,
will burn this sucker right off,"
she shakes the can
like a whipped cream container,
or the nitrous oxide canisters
we called, "hippie crack,"
at Grateful Dead shows.

"This may sting a bit," she warns.

"Let it sting all it wants,"
I tell her, relieved, grateful
my body hasn't betrayed me yet.

Music at the Dentist's Office

Before he numbs me up,
the periodontist asks,
"What music do you want?"
to take my mind off
the dreadful things
he's about to do to me.

"The Grateful Dead," I reply.

"Who are they?"
his young assistant demands,
and hands him a syringe
longer than a Bowie blade.

"A jam band," he explains,
and still she shrugs; I feel
terminally old, but correct him,

" *The* jam band," then lecture
on the medieval folktale
their name comes from:
partly, because I'm a pedant;

but more, because as long
as I keep talking, I won't
have to cringe at the needle's
pinch, then suffer the crunch

and crack of the tooth he'll yank:
a deep sea fisherman turning
a live, glorious marlin
into a dead trophy,

while "Uncle John's Band"
wafts me back to the old Fillmore,
when I had all my teeth
and the night was painless
with music and dancing.

Seeing the Dead in the Daily Crossword Puzzle

I love those *New York Times* crossword mornings
when a clue teases me about the Grateful Dead,
like the Saturday labyrinth, when Will Shortz
smirked, "Dead Bobby," or on the softball
simple Monday puzzle, he lobbed:
"Fill in the blank after 'Uncle John's...'"

I'm grateful the band's entered the culture,
though to watch the stare—blank as a turned
off computer screen—on the bank teller
who asked me about my Grateful Dead t-shirt,
you'd think they'd never existed:

the way memory works, or doesn't,
in America where news is forgotten
in less than twenty-four hours,
and if something hasn't happened
in the past two weeks, it might as well
be ancient and irrelevant history.

She scrunched up her forehead at the magic—
to me—words, "The Grateful Dead,"
then shuddered at the mention of "Dead,"
shrugged, and counted out my bills.

At least, the *New York Times* remembers,
along with all the less significant news it prints.

In the Men's Locker Room at the University of Denver

Rec Center

At the end of my locker row,
two young men are dressing.
One lets it drop like the name
of a world-famous celebrity
that he's Secret Service:
in Denver ahead of
the presidential debate.

The other goes silent
in the presence of a god,
then peppers him with questions,
including the big one:

"Did you ever have to kill
someone in the line of duty?"

His smile's coy as a teen
who wants it known
he's no longer a virgin,
without having to say so,
just that knowing twist
of his lips to indicate
he's a man, a real man.

Collecting my bag,
my ancient Grateful Dead cap,
and the book I'll read
while waiting for my wife,
I glimpse at them again:

both staring stone-eyed
at my grinning-skulled
tattered cap: no telling
what dangerous
radical element I belong to
and what I'm really
doing in Denver.

Insomniac Nights

I suppose I should be grateful
for the tooth-grinding alertness,
the pathetic attempts
to count something—
like the NBA players
who've scored more
than 20,000 points,
or song titles and lyrics
by the Grateful Dead—

and thus induce sleep
to mist over me
like a movie dream sequence.

Those nights don't visit often,
far less frequently than cops
on the take who used to drop in
with large, outstretched palms
on my dad's Lower East Side
millinery factory, whose long,
slow crash kept him up nights.

My sleepless nights remind me
to count my blessings:
that I'm still here, still awake,
still aware most of the time,
still remember the music
of my youth, and can still
lie beside my softly
breathing, beautiful wife.

Professional Courtesy

We pull into a truck stop sandwich shop
along I-25, driving home to Denver.
Four kids lean against an old beater,
eyeing our car as if a delicacy
they'll pry open like a king crab.

Their "black widow," "scorpion,"
and "stiletto" tattoos a, "Screw you,"
to the world, the kids sneer in our direction:
useful only to be robbed and left for dead.

I want to move the car to the building's front,
but fear that will only whet their appetite,
so Beth and I rush inside, exhausted
from our long trip, only half over,
and hurry out to eat in the car.

But they're gone and the car's intact: no
window smash-and-grab, no jimmying
the lock for the new CD-iPod-player-radio
that can pull in stations from Antarctica,
no spiteful crowbarring the windshield,
no syphoning off our gas, or boosting
the luggage we'd left in the trunk: just
a note fluttering under one wiper blade.

"Cool Dancing Bear decals. Keep
on Truckin', old dudes."

Beth and I grateful to be saved by the Dead.

A Near Collision at a Denver Post Office

The kid in the blindingly new
and rhinoceros huge SUV
cuts me off in my old Toyota
for the line to the drive-up mailboxes,
where he studies each envelope
as if for rare Civil War stamps.

I'd karate chop my horn,
but for his "Obama-Biden"
bumper sticker, the Grateful Dead
Dancing Bears decals conga-lining
across his rear windshield:
their jaunty kaleidoscopes
never failing to raise a smile,
for the whimsy
of that psychedelic chorus line.

No sense making the day
worse than it has to be,
on this t-shirt First of December,
when snow should be falling
to save our fragile planet
from boiling over, drying up.

Finally, he drives off,
and I drop in my letters.
The first notes of "Dark Star"
flutter in my head: tentative
as snowflakes, as butterflies
setting off on their epic,
heroic journeys.

The Youngest Person in the Room

The late Jerry Garcia once said
that if everyone else was wearing
suits and ties, he always felt
like the youngest person in the room.

Maybe it was his jeans, sneakers,
t-shirts; and that he made his living
playing a guitar and singing;

not as a doctor, lawyer, accountant,
or the other professions parents
drummed into us were acceptable
ways of filling our bellies
and keeping roofs
over our anxious heads,

when we saw them whispering,
and knew exactly what they meant
without hearing a single one
of their frightened words.

Still, I know what Garcia meant:
youth harder to let go of
than a fat wallet we know
belongs to someone else.

Yet we must.

The Clothes We Never Wear

A friend once advised,
"If you haven't worn it
in five years, give it away."
Sound advice. But some
I could no more part with
than I could my tongue:
clothes I've inherited from
my father-in-law and father.

Like Albear's car coat.
Every so often I'll try it on.
"You look," I'll grimace,
"like a fat banker from the Fifties."

Still, whenever charities call,
I still see or smell or sense
my father-in-law
in its sleeves and pockets.

The same with my Dad's
exquisite silk ties,
though the only tie I wear—
the time or two a year one's required—
was designed by Jerry Garcia,
about whom my father once shouted,

"Turn that crap off
and come play gin with me!"

And yet, from time to time,
I hold his ties before a mirror, and ask,
"How come, Dad, you looked
so smart in these, and I'm a kid
playing dress up?"

I know I won't get an answer,
so I return them to their rack,
almost hear them thank me
for not forgetting altogether.

Funeral Suit

First, it was my interview suit,
then it metamorphosed into
my wedding suit, then the suit
I wore to friends' and family's
kids' bar and bat mitzvahs.

Now I wear it to funerals:
too many of late, and no chance
the last one will be the last.

Most likely, it'll be the suit
I'm buried in, unless I request
a Grateful Dead t-shirt.
But since I won't really be there,
it won't bother me what I wear.

And maybe someone else
can get some good use
out of that suit: charcoal,
with a natty pinstripe pattern,
something my father won't
roll his eyes at, at his son's
utter indifference to good taste,

when, in my fantasies, I'd join
him and Mom in whatever heaven
there is; because if I was wearing
that dancing skeleton t-shirt,
the first thing he'd say
after he kissed and hugged me
a long, long time at so precious
and belated a reunion, would be:

"For God's sake, you're in Heaven,
couldn't you find something
a little more appropriate to wear?"

The Jerry Garcia Stuffed Toys

Along with Petey the Panda,
Pasqual the irascible French Penguin,
and the other stuffed animals
who rest on our bed and talk to us,
there are the two Jerry Garcia dolls,

"The Jerrys," we call them:
one a gift from my brother,
the other from a friend.
Both Jerrys are fiends for silent
jamming and of course, for grass.

Both bear a striking resemblance
to Captain Trips himself, down
to the missing joint——no pun intended——
on his right-middle finger: the result
of a childhood accident with an ax.

When I look at the Jerrys——even knowing
they'll never answer back, or sing,
or flick off some wicked riffs
on their cardboard guitars——I recall
my youth, all things possible,
despite the brute cacophony of Vietnam:

the Dead alive and playing the Fillmore,
tickets cheap as a movie, the show lasting
longer, and never a bad performance.

Staring

The counter-kid at the bagel shop
stares at my baseball cap's lightning
flash Grateful Dead logo.
Not the most dignified headgear,
compared to the fedoras my dad wore

stylish as Cagney or Cary Grant,
but it keeps the sun off, and I still smile
when I hear the words "Grateful"
and "Dead" in the same sentence.
And I can see this kid wants

to ask me something, like,
"Did you ever go to a show?"
and, "What was it like?" and finally,
"Were they really that good?"
By the looks of him, he wasn't alive

when the heart attack felled Garcia,
his ashes flung into the air,
like the flesh vultures take
in a sky burial. Part of me wants
to tell him, "Ask away,"

the other part wants to get home
with my bagel, late for lunch, hungry,
and I know Garcia, with his insatiable
appetites, would've understood:
life's too short to wait for anything.

About the Author

Robert Cooperman was born and raised in Brooklyn, New York, and received a BA from Brooklyn College, whose bogus and interminable football fight song he and college friends love to inflict on unsuspecting acquaintances. In 1974 Cooperman enrolled at the University of Denver, where he earned a Ph.D. in Creative Writing and 19th Century British Literature. Since then, Cooperman has published 18 poetry collections, most recently *Draft Board Blues* (FutureCycle Press), which was named one of Ten Great Reads by Colorado authors of 2017 by *West Word Magazine*. *In the Colorado Gold Fever Mountains* (Western Reflections Books) won the Colorado Book Award for Poetry in 2000. *My Shtetl* won the Holland Prize from Logan House Books. Also, forthcoming in late 2018 is *Their Wars*, from Aldrich Press. Cooperman lives in Denver with his wife Beth.

Acknowledgments

The author wishes to thank the editors of the following journals, where the poems listed below were first published, some in earlier form.

"Music at the Dentist's Office"	*Nerve Cowboy*
"Staring"	*Nerve Cowboy*
"A Near Collision at a Denver Post Office"	*Old Red Kimono*
"The Jerry Garcia T-Shirt"	*Talking River Review*
"Marijuana Sauce, II"	*Tribeca Review*
"'And We Bid You Goodnight'—The Fillmore East"	Twentieth Annual Grateful Dead Scholars Caucus

Other Books from Liquid Light Press

All books are available directly from *liquidlightpress.com* or from any of the current major global distribution channels including Amazon, Barnes and Noble, the iBookstore and the Ingram Catalog.

- ♥ *Leaning Toward Whole* by M. D. Friedman (2011) — Explores the poignant and personal. Also available as a groundbreaking multimedia enhanced e-book.
- ♥ *The Miracle Already Happening – Everyday Life with Rumi* by Rosemerry Wahtola Trommer (2011) — A special collection of poems full of heart, humor, peace and wisdom.
- ♥ *Spiral* by Lynda La Rocca (2012) — A compelling poetic and melodic discourse of the persistent cravings and fears inside of each of us.
- ♥ *From the Ashes* by Wayne A. Gilbert (2012) — A true masterpiece that gnaws at the heart with universal appeal.
- ♥ *ah* by Rachel Kellum (2012) — This poetry has a simplicity and clarity that cuts to the core of being human.
- ♥ *Catalyst* by Jeremy Martin (2012) — *Catalyst* may just launch you on a fiery ride into yourself.
- ♥ *Of Eyes and Iris* by Erika Moss Gordon (2013) — Beautiful yet poignant in its simplicity.
- ♥ *Your House Is Floating* by Susan Whitmore (2013) — As smooth, crisp and satisfying as olive oil on fresh garden greens.
- ♥ *Nowhere Near Morning* by Jeffrey M. Bernstein (2013) — An intimate embrace of what it means to be alive.
- ♥ *Harmonica* by Cecele Allen Kraus (2014) — *Harmonica* bristles with a shimmering music that heals the heart.
- ♥ *Surf Sounds* by Roger Higgins (2014) — Expertly crafted and superbly written, pulsing with the tides of the soul.
- ♥ *Black-Footed Country* by Lindsay Wilson (2015) — Like eating an artichoke, there are layers within thorny layers, each one more tender and subtle until you feast on the heart inside.
- ♥ *The Dice Throwers* by Douglas Cole (2015) — *The Dice Throwers* shines like a flashlight across the gritty dark alleys of the American soul, turning shattered glass into diamonds.
- ♥ *Lessons on Sleeping Alone* by Megan E. Freeman (2015) — While easily accessible, Megan's elegant writing is complexly layered with hard-won common sense and clarity.
- ♥ *The Offering* by Eleanor Kedney (2016) — A masterful, poetic tapestry woven from what makes us human.
- ♥ *This Town, Poems of Correspondence* by Kyle Laws & Jared Smith (2017) — This gifted collaboration on small town America between two of Colorado's finest poets will hit you where you live.
- ♥ *Pneuma* by Jennifer Lothrigel (2017) — *Pneuma* navigates the intuitive world of the self with both power and subtle grace.

www.ingramcontent.com/pod-product-compliance
Lightning Source LLC
Chambersburg PA
CBHW021915040426
42447CB00007B/876